Germans in Michigan

DISCOVERING THE PEOPLES OF MICHIGAN
Arthur W. Helweg and Linwood H. Cousins, Series Editors

Ethnicity in Michigan: Issues and People
Jack Glazier, Arthur W. Helweg

French Canadians in Michigan
John P. DuLong

African Americans in Michigan
Lewis Walker, Benjamin C. Wilson, Linwood H. Cousins

Albanians in Michigan
Frances Trix

Jews in Michigan
Judith Levin Cantor

Amish in Michigan
Gertrude Enders Huntington

Italians in Michigan
Russell M. Magnaghi

Germans in Michigan
Jeremy W. Kilar

Poles in Michigan
Dennis Badaczewski

Dutch in Michigan
Larry ten Harmsel

Asian Indians in Michigan
Arthur W. Helweg

Discovering the Peoples of Michigan is a series of publications examining the state's rich multicultural heritage. The series makes available an interesting, affordable, and varied collection of books that enables students and lay readers to explore Michigan's ethnic dynamics. A knowledge of the state's rapidly changing multicultural history has far-reaching implications for human relations, education, public policy, and planning. We believe that Discovering the Peoples of Michigan will enhance understanding of the unique contributions that diverse and often unrecognized communities have made to Michigan's history and culture.

Germans in Michigan

Jeremy W. Kilar

Michigan State University Press

East Lansing

♾ The paper used in this publication meets the minimum requirements
of ANSI/NISO Z39.48-1992 (R 1997) (Permanence of Paper)

Michigan State University Press
East Lansing, Michigan 48823-5202
Printed and bound in the United States of America

08 07 06 05 04   1 2 3 4 5 6 7 8 9 10

LIBRARY OF CONGRESS CATALOGING-IN-PUBLICATION DATA
Kilar, Jeremy W.
Germans in Michigan / Jeremy W. Kilar.
p. cm. — (Discovering the peoples of Michigan)
ISBN 0-87013-619-4
1. German Americans—Michigan—History. 2. German Americans—Cultural assimilation—Michigan. 3. Immigrants—Michigan—History. 4. Michigan—Ethnic relations.
5. Michigan—Social conditions. I. Title. II. Series.
F575.G3 K45 2001
305.83'10774—dc21
                                                        2001006359

Discovering the Peoples of Michigan. The editors wish
to thank the Kellogg Foundation for their generous support.

Cover design by Ariana Grabec-Dingman
Book design by Sharp Des!gns, Inc.

COVER PHOTO: Matilda and Julius Schubert were pioneer German settlers
in East Saginaw's large German neighborhood. This photo was taken in
their backyard around 1900. Courtesy of Connie Hartley.

Visit Michigan State University Press on the World Wide Web at:
www.msupress.msu.edu

To my family, Mignon, Annalisa,
and Stephen; and to my friends and mentors
William T. Bulger and Henry F. Vassel

ACKNOWLEDGMENTS

The city of Detroit, where I grew up, and the Saginaw Valley, where I have lived for several decades, deserve recognition for their cultural mix that instilled within me an appreciation for Michigan's ethnic heritage. My best friends in my youth were Italian, Polish, German, and Irish children in my west side neighborhood. These ethnic associations continued within the rich cultural heritage of the Saginaw Valley's cities and farms. My professors at the University of Detroit, Central Michigan University, and the University of Michigan consistently encouraged, directly and indirectly, a more insightful appreciation of the state's cultural diversity. Finally, semester after semester my students at Delta College have brought fresh new insights into what it means to be a product of the American immigrant experience. For this past, I am grateful.

SERIES ACKNOWLEDGMENTS

Discovering the Peoples of Michigan is a series of publications that resulted from the cooperation and effort of many individuals. The people recognized here are not a complete representation, for the list of contributors is too numerous to mention. However, credit must be given to Jeffrey Bonevich, who worked tirelessly with me on contacting people as well as researching and organizing material.

The initial idea for this project came from Mary Erwin, but I must thank Fred Bohm, director of the Michigan State University Press, for seeing the need for this project, for giving it his strong support, and for making publication possible. Also, the tireless efforts of Keith Widder and Elizabeth Demers, senior editors at Michigan State University Press were vital in bringing DPOM to fruition. Keith put his heart and soul into this series, and his dedication was instrumental in its success.

Otto Feinstein and Germaine Strobel of the Michigan Ethnic Heritage Studies Center patiently and willingly provided names for contributors and constantly gave this project their tireless support.

My late wife, Usha Mehta Helweg, was the initial editor. She meticulously went over manuscripts. Her suggestions and advice were crucial. Initial typing, editing, and formatting were also done by Majda Seuss, Priya Helweg, and Carol Nickolai.

Many of the maps in the series were drawn by Fritz Seegers while the graphics showing ethnic residential patterns in Michigan were done by the Geographical Information Center (GIS) at Western Michigan University under the directorship of David Dickason. Additional maps have been contributed by Ellen White.

Russell Magnaghi must also be given special recognition for his willingness to do much more than be a contributor. He provided author contacts as well as information to the series' writers. Other authors and organizations provided comments on other aspects of the work. There are many people that were interviewed by the various authors who will remain anonymous. However, they have enabled the story of their group to be told. Unfortunately, their names are not available, but we are grateful for their cooperation.

Most of all, this work is a tribute to the writers who patiently gave their time to write and share their research findings. Their contributions are noted and appreciated. To them goes most of the gratitude.

ARTHUR W. HELWEG, *Series Co-editor*

Contents

William and Alvinia Schnettler's wedding, 1910. Left to right: Fred Peters and Emma Zube, Charles Zube and Lena DuRussell, William Zube and Helda Pett, and the bride and groom. The farmhouse remains standing at the corner of Finn and German Roads near Munger. Courtesy of Duff Zube.

Germans in Michigan

Introduction: German Assimilation Patterns

Jacobine Fass wrote home to Dietlingen, Baden, in 1855: "I never imagined that I would like it here as much as I do. It is very nice here, the nice field and the nice river flows past. . . . I was not homesick." Her new home was along the Tittabawassee River near Saginaw, and like so many transplanted Germans, she readily adapted to her new surroundings. Jacobine represented those German settlers—by far the vast majority—who struggled to become Americans. At this same time, not far away in the Saginaw Valley, the German Lutheran missionary colonies of Frankenmuth, Frankenlust, Frankenhilf, and Frankentrost were also settled. They, however, perpetuated their German culture and remained isolated, self-contained, rural, ethnic communities for over a century. As late as 1950, these towns nurtured a social, economic, and political conservatism where German language, culture, and Lutheranism still flourished.[1]

This latter image of social isolation—reinforced by efforts to attract tourists to "Bavarian villages"—is the stereotype that often identifies Germans in Michigan. In reality there is limited unity among German Americans. In comparison to other immigrant groups discussed in these volumes—like the Poles, Finns, or Italians—there is little widespread interest in preserving a common German heritage. Because they were so diverse in origin, religion, political beliefs, and occupational pursuits, generalizations about the Germans are difficult. Moreover, in the twentieth century, two world wars fought against Germany encouraged assimilation as well as isolation among German Americans. Some withdrew into ethnic enclaves; others eagerly divested themselves of things German and became Americans. Diversity and fragmentation of German society challenges those who write a common history of German settlement in Michigan. Generalizations must be drawn carefully; stereotypes are often inaccurate; and, the history of German settlement is long and complicated.

Despite the popularized representation of rural ethnic isolation, most Germans have assimilated into the cultural mainstream. The ethnic tie to a small clan that created social isolation and nativist resentment is largely extinguished. Ethnic consciousness, when it does exist, is often selective. German characteristics are celebrated both for tradition but also for economic reasons. Ethnic awareness, though,—the praise of retaining German ethnic consciousness—should be approached with caution. By far, most German American immigrants in Michigan sacrificed and struggled to provide their children with a sense of belonging, often for their entire lives.

Once their children and grandchildren mastered the English language, secured steady employment, and transcended narrow parochialism, then they could proudly remember German origins. However, to engage in ethnic sentimentality, as Alan Wolfe reminds us, "is to celebrate a people for what they tried to escape," and "demeans the importance of what they wanted to become."[2] Michigan's German settlers should be viewed as descendants of those who struggled to become Americans.

The contradictory image between cultural preservation and assimilation among German-speaking peoples is best explained by the large number of German immigrants and their places of origin. Between 1820 and 1900 nearly five million immigrants from Germany settled in the United States. In 1920, approximately 18.3% of Michigan's population claimed German birth or ancestry. Between World War I and 1963, German arrivals outnumbered those from any other country. The large

Figure 1. Sources of German immigration to Michigan.

numbers of German immigrants simply made it inevitable that sizeable populations would readily Americanize.

Genealogists, historians, and others who examine nineteenth century census data are reminded that Germany as a unified country did not exist until 1871. German immigrants to Michigan listed their place of birth not as "Germany," but as Bavaria, Westphalia, Baden, Prussia, Mecklenburg, and Wurttemberg.[3] Facile generalization about Germans are difficult because of these provincial differences. Religion, language, social, and cultural variations emanating from varied origins created a truly heterogeneous ethnic group. There was more to being "German" than speaking an apparent common language.

Census data also reveals that many German communities moved en masse; or, individual immigrant leaders built communities in Michigan populated by fellow provincials. For example, Schwaben (southwestern Bavaria) settlers were the vanguard of eventually five to six thousand German immigrants who pioneered in Ann Arbor and Washtenaw County in the 1830s and 1840s. Catholics from Westphalia in the late 1830s settled along the Grand River in Westphalia, Clinton County. Lutherans from Franconia (northern Bavaria) in the 1840s established Indian missions in Frankenmuth and the other "Franken" settlements in Saginaw County. Fifty families from Saxony purchased land and became prosperous farmers near Forestville in Sanilac County in 1873. Several families from Dusseldorf established farms in the Upper Peninsula near Marquette in 1862.

Michigan also attracted many transplanted Russian Germans who came in the 1870s. The list of such communities could extend to several other settlements. What is evident, though, is that common regions, villages, or even neighborhoods in Germany often bound immigrants together. Provincial commonality also meant religious unity and these forces often combined, especially in Michigan's rural areas, to sustain common ethnic-religious identity.

In contrast to rural isolation, life in Michigan's cities, especially communities like Detroit and Saginaw, could be dramatically different. German Americans were the single largest foreign-born group living in these cities in the 1890s. And, although historical generalizations of urban German immigrants imply that most were skilled laborers or craftsmen experiencing upward social mobility and assimilation, that is true of only about one-third of the Germans in Detroit in the late nineteenth century. Germans were well represented in the merchant classes and as white collar office workers; however, fully 58% remained industrial laborers in Detroit's factories.[4] Assimilative experiences in the cities remained contradictory. Some Germans spread across the social spectrum and distributed themselves both economically and geographically among the classes. Still others, commonly factory workers, remained clustered in German neighborhoods on Detroit's and Saginaw's east side and isolated themselves from other Americans.

By 1920 the German community in Detroit lost its geographical closeness, and even working-class neighborhoods disappeared as the Germans moved up and began to blend in with other immigrants and native-born Americans. Urbanization fragmented the German ethnic community and encouraged assimilation.

The fragmentation that the German immigrants experienced in Michigan's cities was often a continuation of the breaking apart of traditional life patterns many had experienced in Germany prior to coming to America. The transition of Germany into the advanced stages of industrial capitalism complicated traditional village life and urban society and prompted many Germans to migrate to the New World. These "push" factors—those forces driving emigrants from Germany— need to be understood if we are to appreciate the nature of the German American immigrant community. Again the German experience evidences a complex association of social and economic factors that affected emigration from the homeland. In fact the common assertion that poverty drove the less fortunate to the New World obscures reality. Moreover, because the Germans emigrated from different regions or districts, push factors varied within specific geographical locations. Some regions experienced larger numbers of emigrants while other sections witnessed almost none at all.

Emphasizing patterns of ethnic assimilation avoids traditional methods of immigrant studies that often simply stressed the contributions of a few prominent immigrants. Collective insecurities brought on by World War I necessitated enshrinement of saintly images of German Americans. This can be seen in John Russell's early history of Germans in Michigan, written in 1927.[5] Instead of focusing on German American leaders and their contributions, the current study will discuss patterns of German ethnic diversity, origins, and assimilation. German settlers became an integral part of Michigan's culture and character, and as such they interacted with other groups in many varied social and economic environments. Individualistic German traditions, culture, and attitudes remain, but they also have contributed to

Figure 2. Wenkel and Peppel family members at Boyne City lumber camp, c. 1904. Robert and Albert Peppel (the two cooks holding the "gaberial" horn) came from Pomerania in 1884 and moved from Pennsylvania to Michigan. Frederick Wenkel's two sisters married the Peppel brothers pictured. Frederick (ninth from right) came from Hamburg in the 1880s and worked as a young man as a laborer and teamster in the several camps. The Wenkels settled as farmers in Standish, Michigan.

the ethnocultural mix of Michigan's culture. The state's character is resplendent in its multiculturalism, especially its German roots.

Rural conservativism, a strong work ethic, and dogged persistence are values that are remnant of the German immigration into Michigan. Anthropologist Sonya Salamon, writing in *Ethnic Communities and the Structure of Agriculture,* affirmed that late twentieth-century German farm traditions have changed little from those of the grandfathers' and great-grandfathers' who migrated between 1840 and 1900. These pioneers were "concerned with continuity and tradition and unconcerned if economic progress came slowly." Salamon makes a point that the

Germanic farmers were not within the Anglo-Saxon tradition of "Yankee farmers" who measured success in "size and profit" and ran their farms as a business. Instead the German family farm was "full of sentiment and made continuity an obsessive priority."[6] These values, brought not only by Germans in their capacities as farmers, but also as mechanics, carpenters, and entrepreneurs, remain a dominant ethos of the state today.

Pioneer Settlement

Michigan was historically identified as a French colony throughout the era of British occupation after the French and Indian War, until English removal in 1796. A few German wanderers and ex-soldiers found their way into the Michigan territory. Most frequently Hessians, German-born soldiers in service to the British crown, remained in Michigan after Jay's Treaty in 1795. Subjects of the crown were permitted to stay in America if they declared their intentions and nationality. After the organization of the Michigan Territory in 1805 and the end of the War of 1812 in 1814, a few individual immigrant families and war veterans of German birth took Michigan land allotments in and around Detroit.

It was not until the completion of the Erie Canal in 1825 and the Michigan land rush of 1834 that significant numbers of German immigrants came into the state. The Erie Canal and Great Lakes' steamboats promised ready and cheap access to the interior from New York City, the key point of entry for European immigrants. Likewise, President Andrew Jackson's war on the Bank of the United States created scores of loosely supervised state banks that now gave easy credit and encouraged land speculation. "Paper" or speculative town sites developed throughout the thumb, and southern and western regions of Michigan. At the same time the relative tranquility within the German home provinces was shattered by religious unrest and poverty after the Napoleonic Wars, especially in southwestern Germany. In 1834 passenger-toll barriers between Germany's provinces were lowered by the *Zollverien* or tariff union. Emigrants could now move cheaply across Germany to the port cities of Bremen, Hamburg, Antwerp, and Rotterdam and begin their journey to America.

The two waves of German migration that occurred between 1830 and the outbreak of the Civil War made the most lasting impression upon the state. These people were not only the first significant body of immigrants, they also became ensconced in Michigan history and made proud contributions both as pioneer settlers and as German American leaders. The initial wave of immigration was occasioned by a missionary effort intended to evangelize both the Native Americans and the growing populations of German settlers. The second wave was most frequently represented by the free-thinkers, or "forty-eighters," who fled Germany following the 1848 revolutions.

Peasants and landless families with few resources made up the initial flood of emigration from Germany. Hunger and despair brought on by the potato famine drove many to seek refuge abroad. The blight started in the Rhineland and spread across eastern Germany. Roads leading from Baden, Wurttemberg, Hesse, and Bavaria were clogged in the mid-1840s with peasants escaping overseas. Whole villages sold their remaining property, rallied around a town official or a local cleric and set off to German or French seaports. Though these people who left were poor, they were not destitute.[7] Many of the people hardest hit by the potato famine simply could not afford passage to America. For that matter, between 1830 and 1850, a higher proportion of comfortable, skilled, and educated emigrants left Germany than in any other period.

As early as 1833, German churches had been organized in Ann Arbor, Detroit, Monroe, and Westphalia. A Roman Catholic missionary writing from Detroit in 1833, attested to the area's ethnic make-up:

Real German life, as it is found in American states, one can find in Michigan only in three places:

(1) In Detroit there a two large German congregations, the stronger being Catholic, the other having a church of its own, being Protestant. The members of the two congregations live in harmony with one another, and never allow their religious differences to interfere with their social intercourse. At marriages and baptisms they are never concerned about which preacher they should choose, but that they should have a good time in the German fashion. A large number of Germans remain in the city only so long as to earn money enough to buy land outside and establish farms.

(2) The second German colony, and the most prosperous is that near Ann Arbor. The Germans there came largely from Wurtemberg [*sic*], and are under the Protestant preacher, the Reverend Mr. Schmid.

(3) The third German colony is that on the Grand River, Ionia County, under the Reverend Mr. Kopp from Westphalia. The colony is called Westphalia.[8]

Frederic Rese was named the first Catholic bishop of the Michigan Territory in 1833. Early in life he had been a Hanoverian tailor and later a soldier under General Blucher at Waterloo. After his ordination to the priesthood, Rese went to Cincinnati in 1823 where he became the vicar-general of that diocese. When he arrived as bishop-designate in Detroit in 1834 the three churches serving the French, Irish, and Italian settlers had not yet been established. Martin Kundig had organized the primary German parish, St. Joseph in 1836, and later was also appointed as Detroit's superintendent of the poor. Bishop Rese also collected support from the Catholic Leopoldine Association, that he had helped organize in Austria, which distrubuted more than $700,000 to the Catholic church prior to World War I. In 1840 Bishop Rese after running into personal and financial conflicts with nearby developing religious houses, retired to Hildesheim, Germany. In his brief tour of duty in Detroit, Bishop Rese had established a Catholic cemetery, St. Philip's College, and the St. Clare Institute, staffed by the sisters of Colletine Poor Clares, to work with the city's destitute population.[9]

It was not only poverty that drove the emigrant, but also hope for a new life distant from an economically and politically changing fatherland. The group of Wurttembergers who settled around Ann Arbor and Monroe in the 1830s and 1840s were Lutheran farmers who fled Germany because family farms decreased in size as land was divided among all heirs. Later in the 1840s, foreign competition drove additional businessmen and artisans to emigrate from Wurttemberg and Bavaria. From the embryonic Ann Arbor settlement in Washtenaw County, chain migration occurred as Lutheran pastors recruited fellow emigrants.

The Ann Arbor religious settlement evolved from the efforts of Wilhelm Loehe, a Bavarian Lutheran minister, and Friedrich Schmid, a missionary from the Basil Mission House in Switzerland. Loehe, an influential preacher in Neuendettelsau, Bavaria, had organized a mission society to train young pastors for work among German settlers and the native Indians in the New World. Schmid had been recommended to Loehe to fulfill the Monroe pioneer Germans' request for a Lutheran pastor.

Upon his arrival in Detroit, August of 1833, Schmid quickly set out to Ann Arbor where he established his missionary base among the thirty-four Wurttemberg families there already. From Ann Arbor he ministered to nearby developing congregations, including the one at Monroe, and worked assiduously to convert nearby Indian villages to Lutheranism. The Ann Arbor nucleus served to attract other Germans who took up farming in neighboring townships. By 1850 approximately 4,102 German-born pioneers were listed in the U.S. Census for Washtenaw County.

In 1843, Schmid was confident enough in his Lutheran pastoral efforts that he formed the Missionary Synod of the West (Michigan Synod I) intended to recruit and train Lutheran missionaries to preach among the Indians. Both the Basil Mission House and Loehe enthusiastically supported Schmid's contributions, and in 1845 they selected Friedrich August Craemer, five farm families, and two single men from nearby Neuendettelsau to sail to America and form a missionary colony north of Ann Arbor.

Craemer, a graduate of Erlanger University, had a command of English and was teaching German at Oxford, England, in 1844, when he was called to lead the missionary colony. Meanwhile, Schmid explored the Saginaw Valley regions and selected an area sixteen miles south of Saginaw as the site for Craemer's settlement. Loehe had already named the perspective settlement "Frankenmuth," meaning the "courage of the Franconians." He had also drawn up a constitution to guide the societal and religious life of the community.

All the colonists reached the Frankenmuth outpost by August 18, 1845. They had purchased 680 acres from the federal government for $1,700. By Christmas they had built a church-school-parsonage log cabin and named the congregation St. Lorenz after the mother church in Bavaria. Although Loehe and Craemer had wanted the settlers to

A Prophetic Voyage

Consider the journey of Frankenmuth's pioneers to Michigan; it is fortunate for subsequent generations that the emigrants saw no portents of imminent failure during and after their trip to America. In actuality their odyssey reflected several of the adversities commonly experienced by pre–Civil War immigrants.

The emigrants left from Nuremberg on 5 April 1845 and traveled by foot, wagon, and train to Bremerhaven. They purchased tickets for a 20 April departure aboard the *Caroline*. While in port, they bought supplies for the voyage. Four couples, compelled by local German authorities, were married. Before they even sailed a drunken captain ran the ship aground on a sandbar in the Weser River. Strong winds and storms in the English channel forced the Caroline to sail northward around Scotland. Unfavorable winds in the North Atlantic drove the ship further northward into icebergs and fog, and during a violent, storm-tossed sea they glanced off of an English fishing trawler. As on so many of these ships, the protracted voyage was wet, cold, overcrowded, and the passengers lacked decent food. Shortly before they arrived in New York harbor, almost everyone aboard was sick with smallpox. A child with the party died aboard ship. Finally they sailed into New York on 8 June after fifty days at sea.

Their trip was not over. After arriving, the immigrants left New York and traveled by steamboat, then rail; as soon as they boarded their train promptly struck a coal train, slightly injuring several of the settlers. Recovering they took a steamship to Detroit and from there a sailing ship took them on a week-long trip to Bay City. The hot, dry summer left the Saginaw River low and they had to pull the ship fifteen miles up the river to Saginaw City.

A few days later several colonists scouted the perspective settlement site along the Cass River. On 12 August when Pastor Craemer arrived with a few of the original colonists, a violent thunderstorm erupted with torrents of rain that thoroughly soaked the weary travelers. The Frankenmuth settlers evidently did not regard this as prophetic. They eventually set about building a church, school, and parsonage, and despite several months of internal rancour, they eventually managed, especially with the arrival of ninety additional immigrants a year later, to establish a successful and prosperous community.

build their homes together near the church, individual colonists disagreed with their pastor and instead lived apart on 120-acre farms. Craemer himself avoided the early communal cabin and lived separately in the parsonage. Early on, the parishioners discussed discharging Craemer as pastor. He was opinionated and rather dogmatic, and the settlers were more interested in establishing their farms than working as missionaries to convert nearby Indians. In time, however, collective animosity was assuaged, and continuing immigration and the rapid growth of Frankenmuth assured a successful community. In 1846, an additional ninety emigrants left Bavaria and journeyed to Frankenmuth. Many of these pioneers led in the successful building of a dam and mill on the Cass River about a mile east of St. Lorenz church, and established there a small but successful business community.

Craemer's efforts to convert the Native Americans met with less success. In Ann Arbor, Schmid had encouraged Craemer to make contact with Indian villages, but the Frankenmuth pastor insisted on having the Indians come to St. Lorenz for instruction. His efforts to change the Indians' nomadic habits and to "Germanize" converts were only somewhat successful. By 1847 only about thirty-five Indians were baptized and the Indian mission moved to Bethany on the Pine River in Gratiot County.

Although discouraged by Frankenmuth's lack of success as a mission, Loehe persisted in founding additional settlements, though their dual purpose as missions and Lutheran congregations ended. In 1847, twenty-two Bavarian families settled Frankentrost, six miles north of Frankenmuth. Loehe now sought to cluster German Lutherans together. Every farm within the community was laid out as a long, narrow ribbon of land so each farmhouses could remain close to its neighbor. Frankenlust, twenty-two miles north of Frankenmuth, and just outside of Bay City, was settled in 1848 along the same lines. The last of the "Franconian" communities, Frankenhilf (Richville), nine miles north of Frankenmuth was orginally planned in 1850 as an industrial center to be settled by poor and unmarried Germans who could not afford Michigan farmland. However, like the others, it attracted more farmers who "had some money and used it commencing the establishment of their homes [and farms]."[10] In all, Schmid, with the help of

Frankentrost, 1847

The preliminary success of Frankenmuth encouraged Wilhelm Loehe's missionary efforts in Bavaria. In 1847, Loehe sent twenty-two new families under the guidance of Johann Graebner to establish a second village named Frankentrost about six miles north of Frankenmuth. Because the missionary value of the earlier effort had mixed results, Loehe's new colony was planned as a Lutheran community, emphasizing biblical knowledge, Lutheran preachings, and the perpetuation of Germanic heritage. Missionary work among the Indians was no longer a major objective of the colony. The immigrants carried $4,000 in American money to purchase farmland. Frankentrost was designed as a village of farms set up in long narrow strips facing one roadway. All of the farmhouses would be close together and residents would cluster within a Christian commune. A visitor wrote to Loehe in 1849: "Frankentrost is a beautiful village, something seldom seen in America. The nice, cozy pastorage sits in the center of the village, and I remember the days with pleasure that I spent there. Sometimes I had to check my bearing whether I was in America or Germany."[11]

Loehe, established German Lutheran churches and settlements in Detroit, Monroe, Lansing, Grand Rapids, Saginaw, Waterloo, Chelsea, Bridgewater, Northfield, Saline, Ypsilanti, Plymouth, Jackson, and Wayne.

Pastor Schmid also established an early German Lutheran settlement in Sebewaing in Huron County in the same summer Frankenmuth was settled. The death of its pastor J. F. Maier, who drowned in the Saginaw Bay, effectively led to the abandoment of the Sebewaing mission in 1850. However, a few years later, in 1857, *Ora Labora*, a unique communal settlement near Sebewaing was established by Reverend Emil Baur.

Ora Labora was yet another manifestation of the dream of an earthly paradise. On the shores of Wild Fowl Bay, in 1857, near Bay Port, Baur, a German Methodist, purchased 300 acres of swampy land and set out to establish a communal colony modeled after New Harmony in

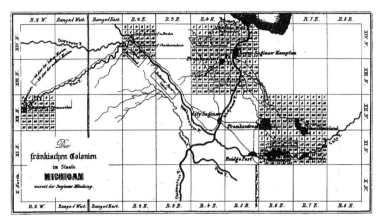

Figure 3. Map of the Franconian settlements, organized by Pastor William Loehe and Pastor Ferdinand Sievers in the 1840s.

Frankenlust, 1848

Pastor Loehe commissioned Ferdinand Sievers to lead a colony of settlers to the Saginaw Valley. In 1848, Sievers arrived from Hanover and established a third German Lutheran settlement named Frankenlust, twenty-two miles north of Frankenmuth. Sievers gathered the Germans together along the headwaters of Squaconning Creek in Bay County. Today this creek is a county drain runing under I-75 near M-84, but in 1851 it was described as a small river, wide and deep enough for navigation by steamers and sailboats. In 1849, a 120 foot-long steamer docked at Frankenlust. Pastor Sievers built St. Paul's Lutheran Church in 1848 and remained pastor until 1893. Frankenlust was another German community that clung to its language and customs, and established a parochial school to maintain German culture. As Frankenlust grew, Sievers' father-in-law, Frederick Koch, located another nearby colony at Amelith and built a residential "blockhouse" dormitory in 1850. Koch served as an agent to bring "contracted" single farm laborers as "serfs" to nearby German farms. A good many of these immigrants later found work in the sawmills of Bay City and Saginaw.

Frankenhilf, 1850

Frankenhilf was the fourth "Franconian" settlement started by Loehe in 1850. Pastor Sievers of Frankenlust purchsed 1500 acres of forest land in Tuscola County, about nine miles northeast of Frankenmuth. The new settlement, unlike the earlier German agricultural communes, was designed as a industrial center and was to be populated by poor and unmarried young adults escaping revolutionary Germany. Bavarian legal authorities, determined to prevent further poverty, began to prevent young couples from marrying unless they had sufficent property or decent prospects of employment. Frustration, poverty, and illegitimate births encouraged Loehe and others to send young people to the Franconia settlements.

In 1850, Pastor Herman Kuhn arrived in Detroit en route to Saginaw; however all but one famaily from his entourage remained in Detroit. The following year a second group of immigrants was sent by Loehe and settled in Frankenhilf, not as industrial laborers but as farmers. They choose the name Frankenhilf, combining Franconia with "hilf" meaning "assistance." In 1851 the colony organized St. Michael's Lutheran Church, which to this day conducts worship services in both German and English. Postal authorities, confused by the difficult name yet aware of the fertile farmland and the prosperity of the German farmers, began to refer to the village as "Richville" in 1862.

Pennsylvania. Called *Ora Labora* or "Pray and Work," the colony grew to several thousand acres with individual German immigrant farmers working 80 to 160 acres held in common. "There was neither riches nor poverty and mankind lived together in continuous Christian harmony." The colony built a sawmill, tannery, and carpentry shops as well as a flour-mill to stone-grind hops and barley for beer. Originally, 288 individuals signed the initial articles of agreement; however, by 1861, the Civil War pulled male workers away, and by 1868, isolation, difficult transportation routes, and the lack of farming experience contributed to a gradual demise of the agricultural commune.[12]

German Catholics also carried out missionary efforts in Michigan. In 1836, Bishop Rese of the Detroit diocese appointed Reverend Anton

Kopp to head a mission in Clinton County. Kopp along with five other men arrived in New York in October of 1836. After taking the Erie Canal and Great Lakes' steamers to Detroit they went directly to the Ionia land office. Kopp purchased 560 acres of Clinton County farmland. They hired a trapper and trader, William Hurt, to guide them to their newly purchased lands. Upon arrival they named the mission Westphalia after their homeland and were soon celebrating mass in their log homes. By 1838, other Catholic immigrants arrived and a log church named St. Peter's was finished. Westphalia was the first German-speaking Catholic settlement in central Michigan. Like the nearby Lutheran enclaves, Westphalia remained a rural, self-sustaining, agricultural village for more than a century. Here, as a county historian wrote, "they are banded together by a fraternal bond that makes them more like members of one family than a community."[13]

Recent research has confirmed that the most important factor determining settlements in America is the pattern, as seen in Frankenmuth and Westphalia, of chain migration. One immigrant cluster or family would write encouraging letters to friends and relatives back home. Those "letters from America" would bring others to an established Michigan settlement and gradually more would follow this chain to create a concentrated community of like-minded immigrants. "Such informal migration, usually by families, constituted the bulk of German immigration."[14]

Much of the chain migration movement, especially to rural and small town settlements in Michigan, was tied to immigrant churches. Though the churches seldom directed recruitment efforts, except for Loehe's Lutherans, new arrivals were of the same religious and sociopolitical disposition. These patterns explain the persistence to this day of certain strong religious affiliations. German Catholic migration to Detroit saw German American clergy dominate Catholic hierarchy in Michigan through the nineteenth century.

The Germans have always been deeply divided over religion, and religious differences inherited from the Old World further served to isolate antebellum German immigrants from one another, as well as from old-line American settlers. Moreover, because many religious communities were peopled by immigrants with money, skills, and

Figure 4. Holy Cross Lutheran School in Saginaw, where instruction was in German until the 1870s. Courtesy of the Historical Society of Saginaw County, Inc.

entrepreneurial experience, immigrants into small-town Michigan were able to persist in self-supporting, isolated, rural villages. As concentrations of German Catholics, and especially German Lutherans with their variety of synods, developed throughout Michigan, each community had less to do with each other. Religious attitudes often held sway over economic competition, and in time many of these little settlements represented religious theocracies where the minister often evolved to become a benevolent overlord. These villages clung to the German language and customs and often established parochial schools in order to perpetuate their culture. As late as 1905, for example, everyone in Frankenmuth (except a Welshman and an Indian) was of German Lutheran descent. Everyone in town spoke German.[15]

A second wave of emigrants left Germany before the Civil War and, unlike the religious settlers, these new arrivals assimilated somewhat more quickly. The new immigrants, or "forty-eighters," were men who fled the homeland as unsuccessful revolutionaries in the aborted democratic uprisings of 1848 and 1849. These individuals were well-educated, politically active refugees who sought to preserve their common German identity in Michigan. Men like Frederick Dieckman, a Prussian

Carl Schurz in Michigan

One of the more nationally prominent German immigrants to America began his early career in Detroit. Carl Schurz is sometimes called the greatest American of German birth. He was born in Liblar, Prussia, and as a college student at the University of Bonn, he published a liberal newspaper and subsequently fought in the uprising in 1848. Following the failure of the revolution he fled Germany to Wisconsin, where he actively participated in the Republican Party's anti-slavery efforts. After serving as a brigadier general in the Civil War, he settled in Detroit and founded a liberal Republican newspaper, *The Detroit Post*. After a few years, however, he was unable to make the paper financially independent despite the support of prominent Michigan Republicans like Senator Zachariah Chandler and James F. Joy. He moved from Detroit to St. Louis and started the *Westliche Post*. In 1869 he was elected U.S. Senator from Missouri, and in 1877 he was appointed by President Hayes as Secretary of the Interior. In 1881 he left politics to become the editor in chief of the *New York Evening Post*.

army surveyor, became a captain in the insurgents' army and was forced to flee in 1848 to Cheboygan and later Saginaw. Carl Rominger a Tubingen teacher who sympathized with protesting students involuntarily gave up his position and emigrated in 1849. He eventually landed in Ann Arbor and became a pioneering geologist. Perhaps the most famous "forty-eighter" was Carl Schurz, editor of the Republican *Detroit Post* in the late 1860s. Schurz later become the first German-born United States Senator representing Missouri and was Secretary of the Interior from 1877 to 1881.

German immigrants to Michigan before the Civil War came because of political instability, religion, crop failures, overpopulation, or land scarcity; but, when seen on an individual basis, each German adult often displayed personal reasons for leaving his or her homeland. Dr. Louis Frank's collection of letters from German immigrants to Michigan offers insight into the complex motives that prompted his family to migrate. For example, John Kerler, a prosperous innkeeper and brewer in Memmingen, Bavaria, was appointed forester. When the revolution came in 1848, his efforts to protect the forest from armed insurgents almost cost him his life and put him under a constant threat of death. Receiving little protection from the authorities he sold his business and resigned his commission. When his invalid mother suddenly died, Kerler saw this as a heavenly sign to depart for America. Like Kerler, most of Dr. Frank's relations were conservative farmers, businessmen, or merchants.[16] Family considerations, religious convictions, and personal needs often determined reasons for emigrating.

Johann Georg Helmreich had come to Michigan in July of 1848, from the area near Bellingsdorf or Nuernberg when he was twenty-six. He and his wife Anna Barbara Hecht were born into large families where they worked as agricultural laborers. Later both Anna's and Johann's brothers and sisters would follow in their footsteps, seeking economic independence in America. The Helmreichs were one of the seven pioneer couples who built log cabins along Squaconning creek and settled Frankenlust. Barbara, who suffered with seasickness long after the voyage was over, was pregnant and gave birth to a son in January of 1849.

The Helmreich's had purchased farmland a short distance from the Frankenlust settlement. It was good land, priced rather low, and located within a mile of St. Paul's Church and the Frankenlust community. With the help of neighbors they built a four-room farmhouse. Johann soon built a barn and outbuildings and added rooms to the original home as the family grew. A smoke house, ice house, and a chicken coop gave the Helmreich's flexibility in diet by allowing storage of meat and vegetables. They canned fruits and vegetables grown on the farm, and raised hogs for such pork delicacies as head cheese, blood pudding, wurst, and many kinds of sausage. Before every meal they said their prayers in German and read the Bible daily. In 1873, Johann's daughter, Marie, took over the farm after her marriage to George Lutz, another Frankenlust farmer. In 1899, Marie died at age forty-nine, leaving the farm to her only daughter, Margaretha, who married another nearby young German farmer Henry Rau.[17]

The Helmriechs may have been encouraged to emigrate to Michigan by the state's policy of recruiting German settlers in the late 1840s. In 1849 Governor Epaphroditus Ransom reinstituted the office of

Figure 5. Albert Zube (foreground) and Charles Zube (rear) on Zube farm, German and Finn Roads, Bay County, c. 1912. Courtesy of Duff Zube.

emigrant agent and appointed Edward H. Thompson, a state senator, as Michigan's Commissioner of Immigration. Thompson traveled to Germany and also to New York City, making arrangements with shipping companies to direct and encourage new arrivals to settle in Michigan. The agency published a forty-seven-page guide book, *The Emigrant's Guide to the State of Michigan,* in English and German. Over 14,000 copies of the brochure were printed and distributed. A decade later, the state appropriated $2,500 to employ additional immigration agents. Two Germans, Rudolph Diepenbeck and George Veenfliet, took the jobs. They opened offices in Detroit and New York and reprinted 5,000 copies of *The Emigrant's Guide,* which promoted the "rails, climate, markets, agriculture, and commercial advantages of Michigan." At the start of the Civil War, Governor Moses Wisner noted that in two years 1,500 German immigrants brought "a cash capital of $150,000" into the state.[18]

The state's recruitment efforts, pockets of isolated Germans, and newly arrived Irish immigrants, began to increase the fears among native-born Americans that foreigners seemed unwilling to assimilate into traditional Michigan culture. By 1850 German settlements in the

Saginaw Valley, Detroit, Washtenaw County, and western Michigan alarmed Protestant nativists. Politicians also feared that monolithic immigrant voting blocs might upset traditional party alignments. At the 1850 convention to rewrite the state constitution, efforts were made to restrict immigrant voting rights. "It is well known," spoke one prominent Democrat, "that there has been a large emigration from Germany and Holland to our State for the last three or four years, and that these immigrants have clustered together and are not dispersed among our citizens." Another politician warned that these "colonies are formed without any mixing of the American population; colonies of thousands; and when they come in and settle the way they do, under the control of their religious protector, . . . you have no influence with them."[19] The 1850 state constitution created a two and one-half year naturalization period for new arrivals; however, this did not satisfy conservatives who sought additional restraints on immigration.

Many old-line Michiganians, fearing alien influences, now joined a new, secret political organization, the Know-Nothing Party. The Know-Nothings, who got their name from their familiar denial of "I know nothing" when asked about attacks upon Catholic immigrants, opposed continued immigration and alien voting rights. The party infiltrated both traditional parties, the Democratic and especially the Whig Party, and was active in areas where numbers of German and Irish Catholics settled. The Know-Nothing Party even attracted some second and third generation German Protestants who moved into Michigan from other areas of the country.

When the political revolution of 1854 occurred and the Republican Party was organized "under the oaks" at Jackson, Michigan, a few Know-Nothing members joined. By 1856, the party all but disappeared and was replaced by the more broadly based Republican organization. The Republicans actively sought to allay the past prejudices of Know-Nothings and recruit German voters.[20]

"Any . . . generalization about the foreign born [voting] as a [monolithic] group extends particularly to the Germans." In the decade of the 1850s, Michigan's German voters were thought to be "in the transition state."[21] The embryonic Republican Party tried to attract German voters, especially in Detroit. German Republican clubs appeared and

German newspapers endorsed Republican candidates in 1856. In 1860, German Americans from Saginaw and Monroe were selected as delegates to the Republican convention in Chicago. "Ethnocentric Germans and patronizing native scholars both established a tradition that the 'German vote' of the Northwest 'elected Lincoln.'" Yet, as Ronald Formisano points out in his study of Michigan's political parties, numerous variables influenced German voting patterns.[22]

Germans in 1860, notes Formisano," remained far more loyal to the Democrats than usually supposed."[23] Those Germans who joined the Republicans were some Protestants and anticlerical rationalists—free thinking "forty-eighters." Still, isolated pockets of German Lutherans remained loyal Democrats. In Saginaw County, the Democrats carried Frankenmuth in 1860. Catholic Westphilia cast 94% of its votes for the Democrats, and in Detroit's German wards Democrats retained control through the Civil War.

Although the party of Lincoln tried to appeal to German voters using them as examples of the ideal, hard working, traditional immigrant—especially in contrast to Irish Catholics who remained Democrats—several Republican stances dissuaded Germans from defecting from the Democrats. Most Germans drank beer and the Republican prohibition stance was uninviting. Moreover, the Germans were not strong antislavery advocates. They probably disliked blacks as a group as much as most native Michiganians. Finally, the Republicans attracted a number of political radicals or "German Red Republicans." These young immigrants, who were staunchly antislavery and anticlerical were repugnant to conservative Lutheran and Catholic Germans.[24]

Despite efforts to politicize immigrants, many Germans remained reluctant to involve themselves in party politics. Edward Barck, a Saginaw resident, wrote to his former pastor in Dietlinger in 1860, that "we are in a way forced to participate in politics, we do so unwillingly as this activity is so crude, even to the highest circles, that it is disgusting." Barck went on; "Corruption penetrates all layers of society and each party tries to rule to have the money-bag of brother Jonathan in its hands. Everything is set in motion for the sake of money."[25]

Edward Barck was "forced" into politics himself in 1860 and became the Justice of the Peace and Saginaw's treasurer in order "to put a stop to the squandering of public money." He remained a loyal Democrat because that party "had always protected immigration," but was unsure about slavery and the principal of popular sovereignty.[26] Barck represented the complexities of German participation in American politics. The fragmentation of German ethnicity—by churches, provincial origins, and settlement patterns—created political diversity. Germans, especially after the Civil War, seldom rallied behind one party. Unlike Irish Democrats, they did not become a monolithic voting block. Consequently, Germans in Michigan were sometimes seen as uninvolved or apathetic participants in politics. Those who criticized German voters' inaction often failed to note that democratic participatory politics had been nonexistent in their homeland.

Volunteering to fight in the Civil War offered German Americans an opportunity to assimilate and prove their American mettle. German Americans spoke at recruitment rallies and many answered Lincoln's call to arms in 1861 and again in 1862. Of the 14,393 foreign-born recruits from Michigan who fought in the war, 4,782—the largest group—were German-born volunteers.[27] The "Stueben Guard" of Ann Arbor and the Michigan Hussars of Detroit were the first two German military societies in Michigan to volunteer for three months in response to Lincoln's initial call-up in 1861. They formed "E" and "F" companies of the First Michigan Infantry.

Their widespread participation in the Civil War on the side of the Union accelerated the politicization of German immigrants. After the war, many German veterans felt that they had a new stake in American society and actively participated in the democratic process. By the last quarter of the century German-born veterans ran for political office and were elected to positions ranging from local mayors, township boards and school boards to the state legislature, the U.S. Congress, and the Senate.

Some Germans, especially those who ran for political office, remained attached to the party of Lincoln because of its stand against slavery and its efforts to preserve the Union. However, as the century progressed, many drifted back to the Democrats because prohibition sentiment engulfed Republicanism, and the party came to identify with Sabbatarianism, belief in the strict observance of the Sabbath, and with

One Family's Journey

Military conscription and the on-going wars of Prussia's Otto von Bismarck drove Johann Zube from Rugen Island in 1865. Located in the Baltic Sea, Mecklenburg, Rugan Island was caught up in the nearby war with Denmark over Schleswig and Holstein. Johann and his wife, Matilda, and five children, Albert, age ten; Sophia, age seven; William, age five; Theresa, age three; and Fredericka, age one, set out on a six-month voyage to America in 1865. The sailing ship leaked so profusely that there were times when the entire family thought they vessel would sink, awash in the high seas. Three-year-old Theresa suffered from an eye infection, and Matilda maintained incessant fears through-out the voyage that her daughter would become too ill to be allowed to stay in the United States. Eventually Theresa recovered, and having heard of the bur-geoning German settlements in the Saginaw Valley, they set out for Michigan. In Bay City Johann settled in as a coremaker with several different sawmills. Matilda had six additional children in Bay City. She died of dropsy at the age of forty-six in 1883, leaving eleven children.

Albert, the oldest son, left school at thirteen in order to supplement the fam-ily income. Like his father, he also worked in the lumber town's sawmills and later in an iron foundry until 1882 when he and his new wife, Alvinia Marzinski bought an 80-acre farm in Merritt Township on German and Finn Roads. Albert soon prospered. He ran a feedmill, purchased a threshing machine, corn husker, and sawmill equipment. He and his equipment were regularly available to his neighbors. Albert and Alvinia had thirteen children, four of whom died young. They kept their farm until 1913 when Alvinia died.

the attacks on parochial schooling. Germans who achieved economic success and became socially and culturally assimilated, especially in urban areas, gravitated towards conservative Republicanism.

Late Nineteenth Century

In the last quarter of the century, the nature of German immigration to Michigan changed. Immigrants now came from northeastern Germany rather than from the south. Peasants, farmhands, and landless workers displaced by industrialization began to move across the Atlantic. Many immigrants were single males seeking to avoid conscription into the Prussian armies during the years of German unification. Others, especially eastern German Jews, became displaced craftsmen as factories emerged and destroyed their livelihoods. Carpenters, tailors, shoemakers, and bankers lost skilled jobs and were forced to choose between the factory or migration to America. The simple introduction of the Singer sewing machine forced thousands of Jewish men and women to work in woolen factories.

Largely uneducated and without worldly possessions, these "lower orders of peasants," were not readily accepted by earlier German immigrants or native-born Americans. Having no savings to purchase a farm and often moving as individuals, male and female, they flocked to the burgeoning industrial cities in Michigan.[28] In 1880 the Germans were the largest foreign-born element in Detroit. The recent arrivals came not only from Prussia, but also from Saxony, Hesse, Mecklenburg, Bavaria, and Baden.[29] Thousands of these northern Germans also flooded the booming lumber towns along the Saginaw River. In Michigan's Upper Peninsula German settlers moved into the Calumet copper ranges and the Marquette area iron towns. Copper was initially extracted by the so-called "German pulverizer" used for reducing soft ores, brought to Eagle Harbor in 1843 by Charles T. Jackson. After the Civil War Germans were initially recruited to work in the copper and iron mines but too often for the owner's interests, the Germans left the mines to run breweries, saloons, and hotels; or, they engaged in other trades. Marquette also was the location of a small band of pioneer Germans who worked in the mines and nearby farms.

Many of the new immigrants from the so-called "lower orders" that settled in the expanding post-war German community in Detroit were the "East Swabians," or "Ostschwabens." The "Reichsdeutsche," or immigrants from Germany proper, considered the Swabians as mixed Germans and thereby of a lower class. The Swabians came from Austria-Hungary's eastern regions along the Danube River and spoke a dialect that was different from the "High-German" spoken by the Reichsdeutsche. The strong nationalism that often existed among German immigrants during the years of the German Empire (1871-1918) brought discrimination against the "less-pure" Ostschwaben or "hunkies" as they were called derisively. Eventually the Swabians created their own community, fraternal groups and singing societies. Today the Carpathia Club remains a Swabian German society in Detroit

Twenty-eight percent of the households of Detroit in 1880 and 39% of Saginaw's were headed by German immigrants. On Detroit's east side—a large area east of Woodward Avenue—German residential neighborhoods were clustered along Gratiot Avenue. New arrivals reflected the complexity of German religious beliefs. About 30% were Catholics, while Lutherans, German Evangelicals, and Reformed Protestant denominations made up the rest. Scores of churches were built in both Detroit and Saginaw. The plain and often simple Lutheran and Evangelical structures contrasted with nearby Catholic edifices that were often built of expensive brick and imported stone. By the turn of the century the socially mobile Germans expanded to other sections of Detroit, even into the long-time Irish residential areas on the west side of Michigan Avenue.

The Germans built simple frame houses on Detroit's and Saginaw's east sides. These cities had some of the highest percentages of single-family houses in the nation, and within both Detroit and Saginaw the Germans owned their homes more than any other group, including native-born white Americans. Home ownership was a way of organizing and perpetuating group identity around the neighborhood and the church. The houses were usually single-story frame structures of four or five rooms built on a 30 × 100 foot lot. In 1897, the mean home value of German workers' houses in Detroit was around $1,054.[30] For German working-class immigrants owning a home was often the sole means to gain security and stability. This stability for a while perpetuated an insulated German environment.

Most of these recent arrivals from northeastern Germany took factory jobs, but many Germans were able to move across the socioeconomic spectrum. Some Germans attained respectable "white collar" occupations within or outside the German community. By 1900, 17% of German heads of households in Detroit were employed in white-collar jobs. Forty-three percent of the Germans worked as skilled laborers

Figure 6. Strable Manufacturing Co., East Saginaw. Courtesy of the Historical Society of Saginaw County, Inc.

while the rest, (40%) functioned in unskilled occupations. Only the Irish, English, and native-born white Americans experienced mobility above this rate. The wage of a skilled German carpenter might be set at around $450 per year.[31]

To save for or build a house, German immigrants like all newcomers worked with both family and the ethnic community. Kinship and ethnicity often enabled German immigrants to survive hard times. The average worker's wage was seldom sufficient to purchase a home in 1900, and many Germans turned to their wives and children to supplement family incomes. The Germans more than any other immigrant group, except Detroit's Polish workers, relied on child labor. "The general pattern for families [in Detroit] headed by Germans was to send children to school between ages of six and thirteen and then to work at age fourteen."[32] Reliance on family enabled the Germans to build or buy houses, finance their churches, and keep local German businesses operating. Limiting the educational opportunities for their children, however, prevented many from advancing and leaving the ethnic community.[33]

Although the Germans began to experience significant upward mobility, the family unit, even in the cities, remained strong. While everyone in the urban household was either at school or working, the father remained the dominant figure. Later, even as children began to marry outside of the German ethnic clan, the nuclear family pattern persisted for a generation. This was especially true in Lutheran and Catholic families where religion nurtured the extended family.

As urban areas in Michigan became industrialized in the twentieth century, it became increasingly difficult for German businessmen and skilled shop owners to compete with large operations. Many independent operators were compelled to become laborers, technicians, or white-collar office workers in the expanding economy. However, industrial expansion also gave enterprising individual Germans the opportunity to achieve wealth and social prominence in the new industrial centers. According to one study, 10% of Detroit's industrialists at the turn of the century were either German born or native-born of German parents.[34]

Information on the background of leading German industrialists is scarce. Like the German community throughout Michigan, sweeping generalizations about these men are often misleading. For example, half of the German industrialists fully integrated into Detroit's Protestant, conservative core of leaders. Men like William Pungs, the owner of a carriage factory; Jacob Siegal, the founder of American Corset and employer of 555 workers;' Frank Hubel, a pharmaceutical manufacturer; Edward Schmidt, a tanner; and Christian Haberkorn, a furniture manufacturer, moved among Detroit's social elite. They built extravagant mansions in the city's prominent neighborhoods and belonged to exclusive clubs.[35]

Other Germans, remained and prospered within the eastside community. Bernhard Stroh inherited his father's brewery on the east side and remained active in German community affairs. Oscar Marx, a German immigrant, not only built the Michigan Optical Company, but also struggled to perpetuate German culture. He financed the *Arbeiter Zeitung*, a labor journal, founded the Harmonic Society, and organized the first German band in the city. Other industrialists like Emmanuel Schloss (clothing), John and Alphonse Posselius (furniture), and Leonard Lawrence (molding company) prospered and remained active participants in the eastside community. For many German

Stroh Brewery

Twenty-seven-year-old Bernhard Stroh emigrated from Kirn, Germany, to South America shortly after the revolutions in 1848. Two years later he left South America and set out for Chicago. On a steamship from Buffalo he stopped in Detroit and decided to settle within the city's German community. Trained as a brewer in his family business in Kirn, Bernhard opened a small brewery on Catherine Street in 1850. In 1865 he bought additional land on Gratiot Avenue and expanded the brewery. His specialty was a new, light lager beer especially popular among the recent German arrivals. Initially, Bernhard sold his Lion Beer door-to-door, pushing a beer-loaded cart through the streets of Detroit's German neighborhoods. When Bernhard died in 1882 the Lion Brewery, which was now the largest brewery in Michigan among 140 other breweries, passed into the hands of his two sons, Julius and Bernhard Jr. Together they expanded the company and changed the name to Stroh Brewery Company in 1902. During the Prohibition Era the company converted its Detroit facilities for ice cream manufacturing, and sold the ingredients for home-brewed beer. By 1980, the Stroh Brewery had become the nations third largest brewery. As Bernhard had in the nineteenth century, the Stroh family consistently put its profits back into the city of Detroit. In the latter part of the twentieth century, the company put $150 million into urban redevelopment projects. In 1985, Stroh closed its Detroit brewery, and in 1999, competition and a declining market share compelled the brewery to sell off all of its beer-brewing subsidiaries. The parent company remained in Detroit and focused on its remaining real estate operations.

industrialists, success came only from operating businesses that remained within and appealed to residents of the German east side.

Business success—the determination to improve their standard of living—is one of the main reasons that German American city dwellers integrated culturally and linguistically into the American mainstream. While not many experienced the Glided Age achievements frequently mythologized in the "rags to riches" success stories, many Germans found significant social and economic mobility through hard work and

Figure 7. Kolb Brewery photo. Courtesy of the Bay County Historical Society.

persistence. This success reinforced the American vision of progress and equal opportunity, and coupled with personal feelings of self-worth, encouraged immigrants to relegate ethnic ties to an aspect of their past lives. They belonged to a thriving entrepreneurial-corporate entity that not only compelled Americanization but total divestiture of any ethnicity.

While not guaranteed, success was often bolstered by higher education and German settlers sought to establish university education in Michigan at an early date. Several prominent German Americans were responsible for incorporating the "Prussian system" into the 1835 Constitution that guaranteed a state-centered educational system. Reopened in 1841, the University of Michigan developed rapidly under the presidency of Henry P. Tappen, 1852–1863. The new president sought to develop a Prussian-like university where emphasis was placed on research and publication rather than the accepted recitation and memorization models currently used. Tappen traveled to Germany and brought Franz Brunnow, an astronomer and the first faculty member with a doctorate, back to Ann Arbor.[36] Bishop Henry Borgess, a native of Oldenburg and head of the Detroit diocese, was influential in getting five German Jesuit priests to establish the University of Detroit in 1877.

Outside Detroit, thousands of immigrants from northern Germany flocked to the midstate lumber towns in the Saginaw Valley. This region remained attractive to Germans because of earlier settlement and chain migration, but also because again, in 1869, Michigan's only Commissioner of Emigration was a German lawyer and real estate agent from East Saginaw. German-born Max H. Allardt set up his office in Hamburg where he published a guide book extolling the virtues of Michigan, especially the Saginaw Valley. *Der Michigan Wegwiser* (*The Michigan Guide*) was distributed in Germany, Bohemia, and Hungary. He encouraged emigrants, many who were industrial laborers, to seek their fortunes among the sawmills of Saginaw and Bay City. Three years later, Allardt wrote Governor John Bagley that 2,722 Germans had emigrated to the state because of his recruitment work. Some, like Charles Ortman and Wilhelm Boeing of Saginaw and the Laderach brothers of West Bay City, built prosperous sawmills. Thousands of others labored in north-

Figure 8. The workmen of Strable's Lumber Yard, 1909. Courtesy of Jeremy W. Kilar.

ern logging camps and lumberyards along the Saginaw River.

Despite the transient nature of their early occupations most Germans settling in rural or small-town Michigan still dreamed of owning a farm. Heinrich Kohn left Leipzig in 1876 at the age of twenty-five. He packed his belongings—pipe, razor, boots, clothes, and Bible—in a wooden crate on which his name was inscribed in English. Heinrich set out for a distant German Lutheran outpost in a place he knew only as the Saginaw Valley. On board the ship he met sixteen-year-old Augusta Tomke who had managed to purchase a cheap ticket from a pregnant women unable to travel. For two years Heinrich worked in Bay City's sawmills to build his savings. He had a simple philosophy, "The Lord hates a lazy man," and he labored six days a week for $1.50 per day. Heinrich lived in a sawmill boarding house as did Augusta. He apparently never engaged in the vices associated with Bay City's reputation as the wildest lumbertown in Michigan. Saloons and brothels lined "Hell's Half Mile" along Water street, but Heinrich worked, read the Bible, and attended German Lutheran services every Sunday. In 1879, he had saved enough to purchase a farm twenty miles outside of Bay City. He and Augusta were married and moved to the farm. A Chippewa Indian family lived in a bark wigwam a quarter mile south of their homestead.[37]

The Saginaw region was also home for a few thousand transplanted Russian Germans. These immigrants were families of skilled German craftsmen who had expatriated to Russia in the latter half of the eighteenth century and settled the Volga and Volhynia territories. Catherine the Great, the German-born empress of Russia, recruited workers to settle undeveloped territory; however, in time they were compelled by the authorities to become farmers. In the late nineteenth century many of these Germans joined the migrations to America. The Volga emigrants selected the Saginaw Bay region, especially Sebewaing, because of its suitability for agriculture. They introduced sugar beets to the valley and many became prosperous farmers.[38]

Volhynia, a province on the Polish-Russian border, experienced a similar emigration of German Russians between 1890 and 1910. These transplanted Germans settled in the southwestern corner of Michigan and became fruit farmers and nursery growers. Berrien County today has the largest concentration of Germans from Volhynia—approximately 60,000—than any other area in the country.[39]

Rural Germans, like those from Russia, and others who lived in small towns remained isolated in closed communities until World War I. Islands of ethnicity persisted and German customs, culture, language, Lutheranism, and German Catholicism flourished. In the cities however, religious, social, and political life became more diverse. German Americans started choral societies, shooting clubs, benevolent associations, and fraternal groups. Reading clubs formed in Detroit and other cities among German elite. Much of this activity was encouraged and sponsored by German-language newspapers. These weekly or daily papers created a feeling of unity within the German American urban community. Detroit had three daily German newspapers in the late nineteenth century. August Marxhausen, from Hesse, founded the Detroit *Abend Post* and later purchased and operated the *Detroit Volksblatt*. Like many German press editors in America, he was a recent immigrant, highly intelligent, and a liberal Republican. These papers emulated the style and content of the English-language press. Although they perpetuated German culture, these newspapers also became effective tools for assimilation. The German press expanded the immigrants' horizons—Marxhausen was president of the Detroit Harmonic Society—and kept them informed of developments in the city and country. In the long run the German American press aided the process of Americanization.

After 1850, and until World War I, Detroit also had many German-language theater productions. Amateur performances began after refugees of the 1848 Revolution settled in the city. A number of these forty-eighters—educated and cultured—organized a *Theaterverian* in the early 1850s. Marxhausen, Hermann Kiefer, Christian Esslen, Casper Butz, and others formed the core of a 150-member society. The Theaterverian put on classic plays by German, Greek, and English playwrights and was active until roughly 1873. There were also a number of amateur companies. Professional companies and well-trained amateur groups continued to perform until around 1900. By then many of the old forty-eighters who had supported the German theater were dead. Production quality declined, and new German immigrants from the working classes had little interest in theater. Moreover, assimilation into Detroit society

Figure 9. Henry Rau and Margaretha with their two oldest children on Franken-lust farm, Bay County, 1909. Courtesy of Otto Rau.

saw a decline in attendance at German-language institutions. Dr. Theodor Boolman started a traveling German theater troupe in 1900 and in that year he visited several Michigan cities. By May, 1901, the permanent German-language theater had all but died in Detroit. Up until the war years, several traveling companies made infrequent guest appearances in Detroit; however, German productions thereafter were limited to special performances by Tunerverian societies and German schools and churches. Still, during this time, German theater served to maintain German language and culture and provided diversion and grounding during the years of assimilation into American culture.[40]

The Twentieth Century

Up until the twentieth century German immigrants often experienced less difficulty adapting to American life than other immigrants. By 1914 those who had come before and even after the Civil War were considered products of the "old immigration" and as such had become real Americans. These Germans were no longer seen as hyphenated Americans but praised as the one non-English speaking group who had "melted" or blended into the dominant, white American culture. Still,

German Farm Life

The weekly routine on the Rau farm in Frankenlust was described in detail during an interview with Henry and Emily Rau in 1996:

After breakfast the men and women would tend to their own jobs. Women's jobs fell into a pattern. Cook, clean up the dishes and try to get something done in between meals. Each day brought a different job: Monday was wash day, Tuesday iron, Wednesday was catch up day and there was never enough Wednesday's to go around. Thursday was shopping day. The ladies would go into Bay City and shop at Zimmerman's, getting the supplies that they needed for the coming week. Friday and Saturday were baking days. The entire fourteen rooms would be filled with the good, sweet smell of home-baked breads. Sunday was church for the entire family. Parents would often join us for dinner almost every Sunday.

The women also had seasonal work to do. Every February, Grandmother would come and stay a week. During this time they would sew all the summer clothing needed. This task would become more difficult as the children arrived. When the weather warmed, the women planted their own garden near the house. They kept busy in the summer hoeing the garden and tending the flower garden. In June when the strawberries came on, some were eaten, some sold, and many found their way into jams and jellies. As each fruit or vegetable came into season, the food was canned to prepare for the coming year. One of the busiest times of the year for all was July when the threshers came. When it was time to harvest the summer grains such as wheat, oats, and barley, the contraptions would clammer along, followed by twenty-eight men. It was the women's job to be sure that the men had plenty to eat. They needed to prepare two meals each day for all of the men. We aren't just talking about feeding them chips and sandwiches. They were big full meals; roast chicken or pork roast, potatoes and sauerkraut, lots of home-made sauerkraut.[41]

rural Protestant and urban Catholic Germans successfully maintained their own language as well as many German customs well into the twentieth century. For example, when Maria Helmreich died in 1899 at the age of forty-six, she left the farm in Frankenlust to her seventeen-

Figure 10. Salzburg Bay City Band, 1910. Courtesy of the Bay County Historical Society.

year-old daughter, Margareth. Margareth's new husband Henry Rau moved into the old Helmriech homestead and together they had seven children. The house continued to grow as Henry built additions until it had 13 rooms. The Rau family spoke only German in the home. They stressed education, and all of the children completed the eighth grade. They said prayers in German before every meal, read the Bible daily, and attended the nearby Amelith Lutheran Church.

Efforts to preserve and take pride in things German experienced a popular revival not only in rural Michigan but especially among German urban intellectuals as World War I approached. German nationalism was extreme and throughout German American communities there was a strong sentiment toward the "Fatherland." The recently unified modern Empire of Germany was as its military and political peak under Kaiser Wilhelm II. Again, the paradox within the German community in Michigan became evident: gradual but persistent assimilation—especially within urban areas—encouraged some to glorify Germanism. These activities often were led by the National German-American Alliance, a loose federation of over three million members in forty states. Originally founded as a league to fight prohibition legislation, it was financed by brewers and led by businessmen, clergy, journalists, and educators. In Michigan the Alliance vigorously promoted the use of the German language, German newspapers, and parochial schools; it gathered considerable support in both urban and rural German communities.

The Alliance, though, could not alter the one factor that consistently worked to destroy ethnic identity in Michigan before and during World War I: rapid, large-scale industrialization. Detroit became America's third largest industrial center between 1900 and 1920, and cities like Saginaw, Muskegon, Jackson, and Grand Rapids matched this pace. German Americans, the largest ethnic group in many communities, could not remain unaffected by the new industrial order of routine and regimentation. Moreover, industrialists, like Henry Ford, vigorously supported Americanization programs. Workers were required by factory owners to attend evening language classes, citizenship training, and industrial education classes. Industrialists thereby derailed "foreign" union efforts and encouraged stability and docility in the work force.

The beginning of World War I in 1914, particularly American involvement in the alliance against Germany three years later, gave industrial patriots a mandate to eradicate any semblance of dual allegiance among German Americans. In Detroit the National Americanization Committee was formed under the leadership of several industrialists—including Oscar Marx, the optical manufacturer and Mayor of Detroit—to promote Americanization and to resist "German propaganda and misinformation, lies, disloyalty, spying, distrust, and intrigue."[42]

The National German-American Alliance came under attack by the Americanization Committee. Early in the war, the Alliance sought to represent Germany's cause and to propagandize for neutrality and against American support for England. It lobbied for an arms embargo, sponsored rallies, collected for German war relief, and organized speakers and writers to oppose American involvement. The German press, German American organizations and many churches, especially in isolated German farm settlements outstate, often opposed American economic support for the western allied nations. However, despite the efforts of these pro-German elements, thousands of German Americans in Michigan shifted toward supporting intervention as war clouds gathered on the Atlantic horizon in 1916 and early 1917.

Nonetheless, anti-German sentiment was already ingrained within the state, and once the United States entered the war, efforts were energized to repress opposition and to Americanize foreign-born nationalities. Rumors abounded about sabotage and disloyalty among the 80,000 Michiganians of German birth. The outpouring of anti-German propaganda had a significant effect on the German American communities throughout the state. Former president, Theodore Roosevelt, said it was impossible for men to be "both German and American." If they tried, "they were not Americans at all but traitors to America and tools and servants of Germany against America."[43] The entire state practiced a form of bigotry previously unseen against a particular immigrant group.

Fanatical patriots attacked German families and smeared homes with yellow paint. Automobiles in Bay City were vandalized, and German flags were ordered taken down from Lutheran churches and schools. There was a public burning of German books in Menominee. Sauerkraut became "liberty cabbage," hamburger became "liberty sausage," and German measles became "liberty measles."

Soon after America joined the war, communities began to drop the German language from their school curricula. Arthur Eddy, a prominent Saginaw lumberman, wrote to the school board, "It is time to cultivate the pro-American spirit. We should talk in English, read it, write it, sing it, and . . . teach only English in our public schools."[44] In 1917 Saginaw outlawed German in the elementary schools, banned books that extolled German culture, and changed the name of Germania School to Lincoln Elementary. Saginaw's city fathers also changed Germania Avenue to Federal Street. German-sounding names and businesses were hastily anglicized. The city of Berlin in Ottawa County changed its name to Marne in 1914 in honor of the French resistence.

The University of Michigan investigated German sympathizers on the faculty. Led by History Professor Claude H. Van Tyne in 1917, an attack was directed against Carl Eggert of the German Language Department for his pacifism and anti-war speeches. Van Tyne received support from William L. Clements, a Bay City industrialist, benefactor, and member of the Board of Regents. Clements and Van Tyne prevailed, and the Board dismissed Eggert. By 1918 Van Tyne was instrumental in causing the dismissal of five other German language instructors at the University.[45]

In response to this anti-German hysteria many Germans withdrew into the ethnic community and also tried to reassure themselves and the state of their loyalty. Lutheran pastors were divided. Some remained committed to opposing the war while others encouraged young men to enlist into the U.S. Army. Congregations compiled statistics that illustrated loyalty. Among many others, St. Lorenz of Frankenmuth sent sixty-two men into the service; Trinity Church in Monroe sent thirty-six young men; and Immanuel of Bay City sent forty-six soldiers. Frankenmuth contributed $250,000 in Liberty Loans for the war effort.[46] The war forced assimilation upon many German churches that now dropped the use of their native language in services. German newspapers ceased publication and German cultural activities lost respectability.

The First World War was undoubtedly a milestone in the history of the nation's and state's German Americans. Several profound social changes occurred that impacted the country as well as the state's immigrant populations. For German Americans the loss of cultural identity was perhaps the most profound, although for many this loss was neither missed nor considered a tragedy. The passage of Prohibition throughout Michigan in 1918 was one war-time measure that deeply affected the state's German populations. Most Germans supported temperance but resisted statewide prohibition on both personal and legal grounds. German-owned breweries, saloons, and beer gardens were common in most cities, and the economic impact of prohibition was felt by the German community in particular. Moreover, prohibition struck directly at German customs and their sense of individual responsibility.

Women's suffrage was another issue that disturbed many old-line German settlers. The German saloon and brewing interest opposed women's voting rights because of the fear that women voters would support prohibition. But many Germans fought the enfranchisement of females on the grounds of religious tradition. German-Catholic pastors foresaw women's suffrage as contributing to women drinking, divorce,

Figure 11. The First Bismarck in East Saginaw's Germania. Courtesy of the Historical Society of Saginaw County, Inc.

and the further breakdown of the family. German Lutherans were opposed to sufferage because they held that a mother's mission was "too sacred to involve public voting and wives would say their piece to their husbands, and their husbands would be taking it to the voters. . . ."[47] Still, such cultural reservations went unheeded. The War pushed strong xenophobic anxieties into a juggernaut that crushed anything that was not definitively American. Prohibition was the law of the land, women got the vote, and the destruction of Michigan's Germanic cultural heritage was nearly complete.

When Heinrich Kohn died at the age of eighty-one in 1932, his admonition to his grandchildren was "Remember to honor thy father and mother." Heinrich had five sons, four of whom lived to adulthood. However, as time passed the Kohn family members began to go their separate ways, and the traditional Germanic ties to the land slowly dissolved. Charley, the eldest who was expected to take over the family farm, "became like an engine that coughs and hacks and knocks and then cuts out when too much is asked for it." He hitchhiked from job to job and beer garden to beer garden. His father took his name off the farm's deed. "Harmony on the farm was diminished."[48] Herman, the second son, bought a farm nearby, never got along with his father, and

The Last Farmer

A GOOD READ

The Last Farmer, perhaps the most insightful account of the inevitable results of the struggle to preserve the traditional family farm, was written in 1988 by a third-generation German, farmer's son, Howard Kohn. Kohn, an award-winning journalist and eldest son, writes of his father, Frederick Kohn, who is confronted in 1985 with the realization that not one of his sons is willing to carry on the family farm. Frederick's grandfather, Heinrich Kohn, had immigrated to Bay County in 1876 and worked in a local sawmill until he could afford to marry and purchase a farm in Beaver Township. Heinrich's son, Johann, worked the farm as did his son Frederick. They carried on German traditions and it was that heritage and the ties to the land that drew Howard Kohn back to Bay County and his father, the last farmer of the title. Kohn Sr. had for years carried on the "old farming" traditions, meaning hard work, dedication to family, church, and community, and little concern for profits. He now found himself struggling against high taxes, foreign competition, inequities in government programs, and children whose time on the farm had come to an end. As its sons wandered off and its daughters married, the old generation stood alone on the land. Though they still had a tenuous affection for home and land, the young people were willing no longer to make the sacrifices necessary for the preservation of traditional rural patterns. In recounting his father's reconciliations and the attempts to preserve a way of life, Howard Kohn writes a vivid story of a disappearing America and of the vanishing culture of the independent, old-time German farm pioneers who settled nineteenth-century Michigan.

simply could not make a go of the farm. After three straight years of losses he found himself quite literally at the end of a rope. The youngest son, Henry, went off to Bay City Business College. The third son, Johann, was the solitary survivor, carrying on the Kohn family farm. Johann's son, Frederick, took over the farm in 1952. None of Frederick's five sons stayed on the farm. In 1985 the farmland was sold. One of Frederick's sons became a nationally known author who captured the demise of his family's farm and its Germanic traditions in his book, *The Last*

Farmer.

The war, industrial amelioration, and cultural assimilation all but eliminated German communities in Michigan's manufacturing centers. Filled with resentment and concern after the war, pressured by industrial leaders who encouraged assimilation, and experiencing economic mobility, the Germans in Detroit, Saginaw, and other towns moved to peripheral residential areas in and around the industrial cities. Yet, by the 1920s most Germans were willing to disappear into American society and culture as quietly as possible.[49]

Following World War I, German immigration resumed despite federal legislation, in the form of quota laws, that limited all immigration in 1924. Between 1919 and 1932, a half-million German immigrants entered the United States. The new immigration laws, despite the animosities spread by the war, still gave preference to northern Europeans. During the Depression years of the 1930s, some post-war German immigrants and "unchastened" German Americans were attracted to the racial superiority and anti-Semitism of Adolf Hitler. It was primarily these people who started the Friends of New Germany in 1932. From its membership the pro-Nazi German-American Bund arose in Detroit in the early 1930s. In Detroit, outstate, and all over the Midwest, the racial diatribes of Detroit's "radio priest," Father Charles Coughlin, attracted millions of supporters, both Irish and German Catholics. Coughlin's attacks on international bankers, his hostility toward Jews, and his isolationism appealed to listeners.

The leading American Nazi in the thirties began his organizational efforts in Detroit. Fritz Kuhn, a decorated German World War veteran, immigrated to Detroit in 1927. He reputedly worked for the Ford Motor Company—although the company claims no record of his employment. The anti-semitism of Henry Ford and his strong anti-unionism contributed to an atmosphere in Detroit that supported hate groups, especially during the union-organizing years among the city's auto workers in the 1930s. Detroit had one of the largest Nazi Bund units in the Midwest. Its members were Americans of "Ayran blood and German extraction" who had to pledge their opposition to "subversive internationalism" and the "dictatorship of the Jewish minority."[50] Fritz Kuhn moved on to New York, and in 1936 he became the leader of the Ameri-

Twentieth-Century Assimilation: William Ortenburger

German immigrants of the pre–World War I era often followed assimilative patterns that contrasted sharply with those Germans living in rural, agricultural settlements.

William Ortenburger was living in Niwiska, Poland, just over the border from Schlesien, Germany, where he was born in 1881. In 1907, at the age of twenty-six while employed as a wood turner, he sailed with another young male companion from Germany destined for Detroit. Instead, they eventually arrived in Chicago where he met and married Sofia Kunicka, a eighteen-year-old Polish immigrant girl whom he had met in Poland en route to Bremen. While in Chicago William played the concertina in neighborhood bars and there perfected his English. Sofia had a son in 1911. Shortly after, they moved to Detroit and Hamtramck where they lived until 1920. William worked as a machinist, then as a tailor, and finally for Ford Motor Company. Around 1920 they bought a farm near Caro. A few years later he traded the farm for a grocery store in Bay City.

During the Depression and World War II, William eventually owned three grocery stores in Bay City and bought and sold real estate on the side. His wife and children worked the stores. William helped his oldest son start a successful trucking business. William also had two twin sons. Edward enlisted in the Army Air Corp in 1941 but was killed on a pilot-training mission in California in 1942. Willard also enlisted in the Canadian Air Force but joined the Air Corps at the beginning of World War II and became a career Air Force officer. Another war with Germany, intermarriage, and geographical mobility all led the initial generation of the family of William Ortenburger to follow assimilative patterns that quickly and completely Americanized twentieth-century German immigrants.

can Nazis. Still, only a small percentage of German Americans joined ranks with the Bund. Unlike during the First World War, German Americans overwhelmingly joined the allied armies. Even by 1939 Nazi extremes had caused the German Bund to "dry up and blow away like milkweed."[51]

During the war, the United States continued to look with suspicion

Figure 12. William Orten-burger with his daughter Helen and twin sons, Edward and Willard. Courtesy of Thomas R. Ortenburger.

upon those of "enemy ancestry." This included not only the well-known example of over 100,000 Japanese Americans who were placed in internment camps, but over 11,000 German Americans were likewise detained. Approximately 300,000 German-born aliens were registered as possible "enemy aliens" in 1940, and of these, many were eventually selectively interned. In coordination with the FBI, the U.S. Army moved suspected German American citizens out of excluded military zones, and detained citizen and non-citizen alike in detention centers, hospitals, and jails for months. Eventually, fifty detention facilties were built, one of them in Detroit. While thousands of German Americans were arrested, excluded, harrassed, and even exchanged for American prisoners in Germany, the U. S. government has yet to publicly acknowledge these violations of civil liberties.[52]

Between World War II and the end of the twentieth century, nearly one million additional German immigrants came to the United States. Because of the war and the divided and war-torn country they left, newer generations of German Americans rarely harbored nostalgia for the fatherland or displayed great interest in their culture. Visible evidence is gone and, by and large, German influences have been absorbed by the larger cultures of Michigan. The Germans, especially the city dwellers, have long lost their ethnicity. German inhabitants of cities and suburbs had already anglicized their names, and even in rural areas the German language disappeared completely in business dealings. Marriages with partners outside of the ethnic and religious identity were frequent and commonly accepted. Except for a few rural communities, Lutheran, Reformed, and Catholic congregations had primarily English-language services and began to call young, non-German pastors to meet the demands of a younger and ethnically diverse population. As one historian recently noted: "There is a direct relationship between the decline of ethnicity and the decline of beer."[53]

The discovery in the late 1960s of the "new ethnicity" has enabled some third- and fourth-generation Germans to revive their heritage. North of Detroit along the I-75 corridor, the old German village of Frankenmuth has become Michigan's "Little Bavaria" and subsequently the state's number one tourist attraction. Relics of the lumber days, hotels and resturants struggled to survive in Frankenmuth under changing ownerships. They provided the foundation for today's highly successful enterprises, operated by Zehnder's Inc. These restuarants and Kern's sausage factory repesent two local businesses still run by families active in the city's formative years. The northern Michigan town of Gaylord also resurrected itself from near oblivion by adopting a Bavarian motif to attract summer and winter tourists. Both cities made somewhat controversial decisions in midcentury to emphasize their German antecedents by adopting common Bavarian architectural styles. While a popular architectural revival style seen in apartment and housing developments, it was clearly intended in Frankenmuth and Gaylord to affirm the German roots of the communities and to set themselves apart from other nearby towns. Today, everyone in Frankenmuth and Gaylord can be German for awhile especially during an Oktoberfest or Alpenfest.

The collapse of East Germany and the reunification of the home-

land in 1990 likewise has sparked a renewed interest in German heritage. The establishment of a reunited and economically strong
Germany as a leader among nations has finally enabled many German
Americans to set aside the ethnic cloud produced by two world wars.
Confronting and apologizing for the Holocaust likewise lessened the
burden of history for Germans and German Americans. A surge in
genealogical research also occurred that has revived interest and pride
in things German. Still, the state's largest ethnic group seems to have
been the last to jump aboard the genealogical bandwagon. While many
other immigrant ancestors have pursued their roots and rediscovered
their history, there have been few scholarly efforts to recapture the
German heritage in Michigan. Doubtless, the ethnic identity of German
Americans has become diluted because of their length of time in
Michigan and by their social and economic success. They have been so
completely involved in the assimilative process that in many respects
they have co-authored, along with the Yankee tradition, the cultural
milieu in which all Michiganians live.

Though there is only a passing revival of interest in German
American culture, in the twenty-first-century Germans remain the
largest ancestral group in Michigan, representing over 2.6 million
descendants or 22% of the state's population. However, less then one-
half of 1% of those with German ancestry speak German at home, less
then 2% are farmers, and fully 60% are in management/professional/
technical/administrative occupations. At the beginning of a new century, some Michigan Germans may still remember their ethnicity, but
most have become thoroughly assimilated into the American mainstream.[54]

Like the entire German experience in Michigan there remains the
paradox between assimilation and selective ethnicity. In celebrating
ethnicity, though, one should not lament the lost German culture but
remember that within the state the Germans rather successfully transcended ethnicity and helped to define Americanism. We should not
forget the struggles and the triumphs of those who paid so dearly so
that German descendants could contribute to and participate in a common Michigan culture.

Notes

1. Jacobine Fass to Pastor Frank, Saginaw, 11 November 1855, in Louis F. Frank, *German American Pioneers in Wisconsin and Michigan: the Frank-Kerler Letters, 1849–1864* (Milwaukee: Milwaukee County Historical Society, 1971), 340.

2. Alan Wolfe, "The Return of the Melting Pot," *The New Republic,* December 1990, 30.

3. The first inquiry into specific places of birth was not made until the 1860 census. By 1870, most Germans in Michigan came from Prussia, Württemberg, Bavaria, Baden, and Mecklenburg. There were 64,143, German-born immigrants in Michigan in 1870; and 135,509 in 1890. John A. Russell, *The Germanic Influence in the Making of Michigan* (Detroit, Mich.: The University of Detroit, 1927), 62–63.

4. Olivier Zunz, *The Changing Face of Inequality: Urbanization, Industrial Development and Immigrants in Detroit, 1880–1920* (Chicago, Ill.: University of Chicago Press, 1982), 338–43.

5. Russell, *Germanic Influence,* vols. 2–3.

6. Quoted in Howard Kohn, *The Last Farmer: An American Memoir* (New York: Harper and Row, 1988), 16.

7. Walter D. Kamphoefner, "At the Crossroads of Economic Development: Background Factors Affecting Emigration from Nineteenth-Century **47**

Germany," in *Migration Across Time and Nations: Population Mobility in Historical Contexts,* ed. Ira A. Glazer and Luigi de Rosa (New York: Holmes and Meier, 1986), 174–201.

8. Russell, *Germanic Influence,* 54–55.

9. Francis X. Canfield, "A Diocese so Vast: Bishop Rese in Detroit," *Michigan History* 51 (1967): 202–12.

10. Russell, *Germanic Influence,* 92.

11. Gunda Hecht Schricker, *The Hecht Book* (Munich: n.p., 1997), 76–77.

12. Chester A. Hey, comp., *Huron County Illustrated History* (n. p.: n. p, 1932), 45.

13. Ronald P. Formisano, *The Birth of Mass Political Parties: Michigan, 1827–1861* (Princeton, N. J.: Princeton University Press, 1971), 184.

14. Frederick C. Luebke, *Germans in the New World: Essays in the History of Immigration* (Chicago: University of Illinois Press, 1990), 165.

15. Russell, *Germanic Influence,* 337.

16. Frank, *German American Pioneers,* 55–56.

17. Wanda Owings, *Rau Family History* (manuscript, 1996), 4–7.

18. Bruce A. Rubenstein and Lawrence E. Ziewacz, *Michigan: A History of the Great Lakes State* (St. Louis, Mo.: Forum Press, 1981), 121.

19. State of Michigan, *Report of the Proceedings and Debates in the Convention to Revise the Constitution of the State of Michigan, 1850* (Lansing: State of Michigan, 1850), 278–79.

20. Formisano, *Birth of Mass Political Parties,* 293–303.

21. *Detroit Democrat,* 11 February1856, quoted in Formisano, *Birth of Mass Political Parties,* 299.

22. Ibid., 300.

23. Ibid.

24. Ibid., 302–304.

25. Frank, *German American Pioneers,* 421.

26. Ibid., 435-38.

27. Russell, *Germanic Influence,* 111.

28. John Bodnar, *The Transplanted: A History of Immigrants in Urban America* (Bloomington: Indiana University Press, 1985), 6.

29. Zunz, *Changing Face of Inequality,* 34.

30. Ibid., 153; Jeremy W. Kilar, *Michigan's Lumbertowns: Lumbermen and Laborers in Saginaw, Bay City, and Muskegon, 1870–1905* (Detroit, Mich.:

Wayne State University Press, 1990), 206.

31. Zunz, *Changing Face of Inequality,* 221–23, 230–31.

32. Ibid., 234–40.

33. Zunz's statistics bring into question many of the earlier assumptions made by historians that German immigrants had a "thirst for learning." George Graff, *The People of Michigan* (Lansing: Michigan Department of Education, 1974), 41.

34. Zunz, *Changing Face of Inequality,* 205.

35. Ibid., 216.

36. Alan Creutz, "The Prussian System and Practical Training," *Michigan History* 65 (1981): 33–34.

37. Kohn, *The Last Farmer,* 78.

38. Graff, *The People of Michigan,* 44.

39. Ibid., 44.

40. Mark O. Kistler, "The German Theater in Detroit," *Michigan History* 47 (1963): 289–300.

41. Owings, *Rau Family History,* 11–13.

42. Quoted in Zunz, *Changing Face of Inequality,* 318.

43. Ellis W. Hawley, *The Great War and the Search for Order* (New York: St. Martin's Press, 1979), 29.

44. Stuart D. Gross, *Saginaw: A History of the Land and the City* (Woodland Hills: Windsor Publications, Inc., 1980), 97.

45. James D. Wilkes, "Van Tyne: The Professor and the Hun!," *Michigan History* 55 (1971): 190–91.

46. Russell, *Germanic Influence,* 340.

47. Kohn, *The Last Farmer,* 135.

48. Ibid., 252-53.

49. Zunz, *Changing Face of Inequality,* 348–49.

50. Ralph F. Bischoff, *Nazi Conquest Through German Culture* (Cambridge, Mass.: Harvard University Press, 1942), 178.

51. Richard O'Conner, *The German-Americans* (Boston, Mass.: Little, Brown and Company, 1968), 451.

52. Karen E. Ebel, "WWII Violations of German American Civil Liberties by the United States Government," German American Organizations, February 2000. *www.serve.com/shea/germusa/societs.htm*

53. Wolfe, "Return of the Melting Pot," 29.

54. U. S. Bureau of Census, "Update of 1990 Census of Population and Housing, Summary Tap Ale 3," February 2001. *www.factfinder.census.gov/servlet/ Basicfacts*

For Further Reference

An asterisk indicates those works especially beneficial for readers who would like to learn more about Germans.

Bischoff, Ralph F. *Nazi Conquest through German Culture.* Cambridge, Mass.: Harvard University Press, 1942.

Bodnar, John. *The Transplanted: A History of Immigrants in Urban America.* Bloomington: Indiana University Press, 1985.

Canfield, Francis X. "A Diocese So Vast: Bishop Rese in Detroit." *Michigan History* 51 (1967):202–12.

Cook, Bernard A., and Rosemary Petralle Cook. *German Americans.* Vero Beach, Fla.: Rourke Corporation, 1991.

Creutz, Alan. "The Prussian System and Practical Training." *Michigan History* 65 (1981):32–39.

Ebel, Karen E. "WWII Violations of German American Civil Liberties by the United States Government." German American Organizations, February 2001. *www.serve.com/shea/germusa/societs.htm*

Formisano, Ronald P. *The Birth of Mass Political Parties: Michigan, 1827–1861.* Princeton: Princeton University Press, 1971.

*Frank, Louis F. *German American Pioneers in Wisconsin and Michigan: The*

Frank-Kerler Letters, 1849–1864. Milwaukee: Milwaukee County Historical Society, 1971.

*Graff, George. *The People of Michigan.* Lansing: Michigan Department of Education, 1974.

Gross, Stuart D. *Saginaw: A History of the Land and the City.* Woodland Hills: Windsor Publications, Inc., 1980.

Hawley, Ellis W. *The Great War and the Search for Order.* New York: St. Martin's Press, 1979.

Helbich, Wolfgang. "The Letters They Sent Home: The Subjective Perspective of German Immigrants in the Nineteenth Century." *Yearbook of German-American Studies* 22, no. 13 (1987):

Hey, Chester A., comp. *Huron County Illustrated History.* N.p.: n.p., 1932.

Kamphoefner, Walter D. "At the Crossroads of Economic Development: Background Factors Affecting Emigration from Nineteenth-Century Germany." In *Migration Across Time and Nations: Population Mobility in Historical Contexts,* edited by Ira A. Glazier and Luigi de Rosa. New York: Holmes and Meier, 1986.

Kilar, Jeremy W. *Michigan's Lumbertowns: Lumbermen and Laborers in Saginaw, Bay City, and Muskegon 1870–1905.* Detroit: Wayne State University Press, 1990.

Kistler, Mark O. "The German Theater in Detroit." *Michigan History* 47 (1963): 289–300.

Kohn, Howard. *The Last Farmer: An American Memoir.* New York: Harper and Row, 1988.

*Luebke, Frederick C. *Germans in the New World: Essays in the History of Immigration.* Chicago: University of Illinois Press, 1990.

*O'Conner, Richard. *The German-Americans.* Boston: Little, Brown and Company, 1968.

Orttenburger, Rick, and Christi Orttenburger. *The Orttenburger Family: A Journey over Countries and Time.* Agoura Hills, Calif.: Orttenburger Publications, 1999.

Owings, Wanda. *Rau Family History.* Manuscript, 1996.

Rippley, LaVern J. *The German Americans.* Boston, Mass.: Twayne, 1995.

Rubenstein, Bruce A., and Lawrence E. Ziewacz. *Michigan: A History of the Great Lakes State.* St. Louis, Mo.: Forum Press, 1981.

*Russell, John A. *The Germanic Influence in the Making of Michigan.* Detroit: The

University of Detroit, 1927.

State of Michigan. *Report of the Proceedings and Debates in the convention to revise the Constitution of the State of Michigan, 1850.* Lansing, 1850.

Schricker, Gunda Hecht. *The Hecht Book.* Munich: n.p., 1997.

U.S. Bureau of Census, "Update of 1990 Census of Population and Housing, Summary Tap Ale 3," February 2001. *www.factfinder.census.gov/servlet/ Basicfacts*

Wilkes, James D. "Van Tyne: the Professor and the Hun!" *Michigan History.* 55 (1971):190–91.

Wolfe, Alan. "The Return of the Melting Pot." *The New Republic,* 30 December 1990, 29–34.

Zunz, Olivier. *The Changing Face of Inequality: Urbanization, Industrial Development and Immigrants in Detroit, 1880–1920.* Chicago: University of Chicago Press, 1982.

German Organizations

There are hundreds of German American societies listed in the United States dedicated to the preservation and study of German American heritage. Rather than including an exhaustive list, the most essential and useful organizations for research on German Americans are listed below.

Several essential web sites that catalogue many helpful German American agencies and resorts are:

- American Association for Teachers of German, 112 Haddontowns Ct. #104, Cherry Hill, NJ 08034; *www.aatg.org/*
- Federation of Eastern European Family History, *www.//feeths.org/ehtnic. html*
- The German Corner, *www.germancorner.com*
- German American Organizations, *www.serve.com/shea/germusa/societs.htm*

German Societies

- Stueben Society of America, Ridgewood, NY 11385
- Society for German American Studies, German Department, St. Olaf's College, Northfield, MN 55057

- Carpathian Club, Sterling Heights, MI
- German American National Congress, 4740 N. Western Ave., Chicago, IL 60625
- Max Kada Institute for German Studies, 901 University Bay Drive, Madison, WI 53705
- German American Heritage Center, P.O. Box 243, Davenport, IA 52805
- United German American Committee
- German Studies Association
- Anglo-German Family History Association
- German-Bohemian Heritage Society
- German Genealogical Society of America
- German Genealogical Society
- German Research Association

Index